IMAGES OF
GLASGOW

A pictorial history of Clydeside's people and places

City of spires and steeples. This view was taken from the roof of the *Evening Times* and *Herald* building in Albion Street in the late 1980s. *1-02*

IMAGES OF
GLASGOW

A pictorial history of Clydeside's people and places

Compiled by
Robert Jeffrey and Ian Watson

First published in Great Britain by The Breedon Books Publishing Company Limited
3 The Parker Centre, Mansfield Road, Derby, DE21 4SZ. 1995, softback edition 2005

Reprinted 2008.

This paperback edition published in Great Britain in 2013 by DB Publishing,
an imprint of JMD Media Ltd

ACKNOWLEDGEMENTS

The assistance of the following people in the preparation of this book is gratefully acknowledged: Jim McNeish, Tom Noble, John Quinn, Dougald Cameron, Jane Westmorland, Tony Murray, Malcolm Beaton, John Linklater, John Easton, Tony Adams, David Belcher, Ken Gallacher, Mike Hildrey, Allan Laing, John McCalman, Jimmy Reid, STV Publicity, Herald and Evening Times Reference Librarians, staff photographers, past and present, of the Herald and Evening Times.

Copies of most pictures in this book are available for personal or commercial use.

Contact Photo Sales Department, Caledonian Newspapers,

195 Albion Street, Glasgow, G1 1QP,

quoting the picture reference number.

ISBN 978-1-85983-665-1

Printed and bound in the UK by Copytech (UK) Ltd Peterborough

Contents

Foreword

by Jack Webster

WE TAKE it all for granted, the commonplace of our daily lives, until it slips away quietly and re-emerges one day under the guise of history. Then, in the perspective of time, we look at it anew and marvel at the significance of what had once been dismissed as mundane.

That impact of reviewing all our yesterdays is never more forceful than in the stark reality of pictures. And the book now in your hands must rank surely as the most comprehensive record of Glasgow and its myriad of images we have yet seen.

Different aspects of the city and its life have found their way into book form but not in such breadth of scope and vision. And for the privilege of this remarkable collection we can thank the incomparable range of *The Herald* and *Evening Times* picture library, a treasure if ever there was one.

Now it is being exploited to full effect. For here you have the pictorial history of Clydeside, from a portrayal of everyday life in all its richness and deprivation to major events and personalities as they have etched their way into the story.

It is the stuff of fascination – and argument. Who remembers what Gorbals Cross looked like? Or where did the old Empire Theatre stand?

There is a generation which has heard great legends of sport and entertainment but could not put a face to the names of Benny Lynch or Dave Willis or Tommy Morgan.

From trams and trolleys to great sporting triumphs and tragedies, here is a century of life in Glasgow and its surroundings which needs to be savoured and fixed securely in our heritage lest we lose sight of it in the preoccupation with modern technology.

What is history if we cannot learn from its lessons? And when you see it in all its black-and-white reality, you gain a balance and perspective, not to mention the sheer joy of recollection which has intrigued human beings since time began.

Pictures affect different people according to their age, experience and perception. Within these pages you may glance at one particular shot and see no more than a column of young Glaswegians marching off to World War One. Only a closer scrutiny of faces allows the imagination to assess the mood of those men – and to wonder how many survived the slaughter of the Somme and Passchendaele to appreciate the rest of their lives back home in Bridgeton.

That war was barely over when the Bolshevik Revolution of the Soviet Union was having its own repercussions in the forum of Glasgow's George Square. Men who came back from war with the promise of homes fit for heroes found themselves instead engaged in the General Strike of 1926, reflected here in workers overturning a local bus.

But depression and poverty ran in tandem with a lively scene of theatre, cinema and dancing. Harry Lauder was opening the new Embassy Cinema in Shawlands, large crowds joined the queue at the Coliseum in Eglinton Street to see Charlie Chaplin in *City Lights* – and the massive Paramount in Renfield Street stood majestic in all its floodlit splendour.

The name in bright lights at the Paramount is Bing Crosby, appearing in *She Loves Me Not*, while the secondary line announces 'Henry Croudson on the mighty organ'.

Throughout that earlier part of the century, too, the theatre was flourishing in Glasgow as elsewhere, great names like the Empire (graveyard of English comics), the Alhambra (trumpeting its Five Past Eight show), the New Metropole ('Ma Logan is Here!') and, happily still with us, the King's and the Citizens', which changed its name from the Royal Princess in 1945.

Straddling silver screen and stage, the memorable Green's Playhouse in Renfield Street once boasted Europe's largest cinema on one floor and a massive ballroom on another before the building became the Apollo, Glasgow's major venue for pop concerts.

Not all the theatres escaped the hazard of fire. In 1953, the Lyric in Sauchiehall Street, which began life as the Royalty in 1879, was destroyed in a blaze. Although it was rebuilt after the fire, it was nevertheless demolished in 1962.

Mercifully, spectacular fires seem less common in these more safety-conscious days. But Glasgow remembers some horrifying examples – the death of 13 shop girls at Grafton's in Argyle Street in May 1949; the 19 firemen and salvage workers killed while tackling the whisky warehouse blaze at Cheapside Street in March 1960, and, largest death toll of them all, the 20 victims grappling with iron-barred windows in an upholstery factory at James Watt Street, their frantic screams receding to a haunting silence on a dull November morning of 1968.

In the flames of destruction, Glasgow also lost its famous concert venue, the St Andrew's Halls, in 1962 and the gracious Grosvenor Hotel in Great Western Road in 1978, later restored to its former splendour by the proud chairman of the company, Reo Stakis.

Disasters of another order claimed more lives in 1971, a year which opened with 66 football supporters being crushed to death on Stairway 13 at Ibrox Park, at the end of the traditional Rangers-Celtic match, and continued with 20 more dead in an explosion at the new shopping centre at Clarkston Toll, on the south side of Glasgow.

But not everything was death and disaster. For Glasgow has housed some of the memorable public events of the century, most notably the Empire Exhibition which drew more than 12 million people to Bellahouston Park in the period from spring till autumn of 1938.

It was Scotland's biggest event, hosting the nations of the Empire in a celebration of their industry and culture, set amid a grandeur of waterfalls and fountains, topped off by the mighty Tower of Empire at the top of Bellahouston Hill.

On that last night, no fewer than 365,000 people endured a deluge to link arms and sing and dance *The Lambeth Walk,* from the popular show of the time, *Me and My Girl.* Little did they know, as they lowered the lights that night, that they were witnessing not just the end of an exhibition but the end of an empire as well.

For by then, the Prime Minister, Neville Chamberlain, was returning from Munich in the vain hope of averting another World War. And when that was over we lit the bonfires of Victory in Europe – and faced a world we scarcely knew. Glasgow was still a city of industrial grime but soon there was cause to lament the loss of that heavy industry. The shipyards which symbolised the world supremacy of the River Clyde faced competition from the Far East and union intransigence at home.

Yards like John Brown of Clydebank, which built the *Queen Mary* and the *Queen Elizabeth* for Cunard before the war, managed to complete the royal trio with the *QE2* in 1967 before the industry all but disappeared.

If there was a consolation for the loss of industrial jobs it was the welcome loss of an accompanying smog. Then a mighty gale in 1968 rocked the rafters of Glasgow and prompted demolition, restoration and general cleaning up of its magnificent Victorian architecture.

On the way to the modern face of the city, this book reminds you of the old Charing Cross, Miss Cranston's Tearooms, Sammy Dow's pub, the Barras, Paddy's Market and so much more.

But now they had burrowed under the Clyde to scoop out the Tunnel, built the Kingston Bridge and the motorway network and celebrated with the Garden Festival of 1988 and as European City of Culture in 1990. In sporting parallels, Celtic and Rangers had already brought home European trophies.

Culturally, the city which had secured one of Salvador Dali's most illustrious paintings received its greatest boost with Sir William Burrell's gift of his unique collection.

To crown all that, Glasgow built a magnificent Royal Concert Hall at the top of Buchanan Street, coinciding with the celebrations of 1990.

It is all here – the face of 20th-century Glasgow spread comprehensively across the pages of this volume in all the stark and exciting variety of history. It was an appropriate accolade that the Dear Green Place was chosen as the United Kingdom's City of Architecture for 1999.

• *Herald* feature writer Jack Webster is one of Scotland's leading journalists and authors. His autobiography *Grains of Truth* was much acclaimed. He is also well known for his award-winning documentary films for television, charting his life from the 1930s to the 1990s.

High Level

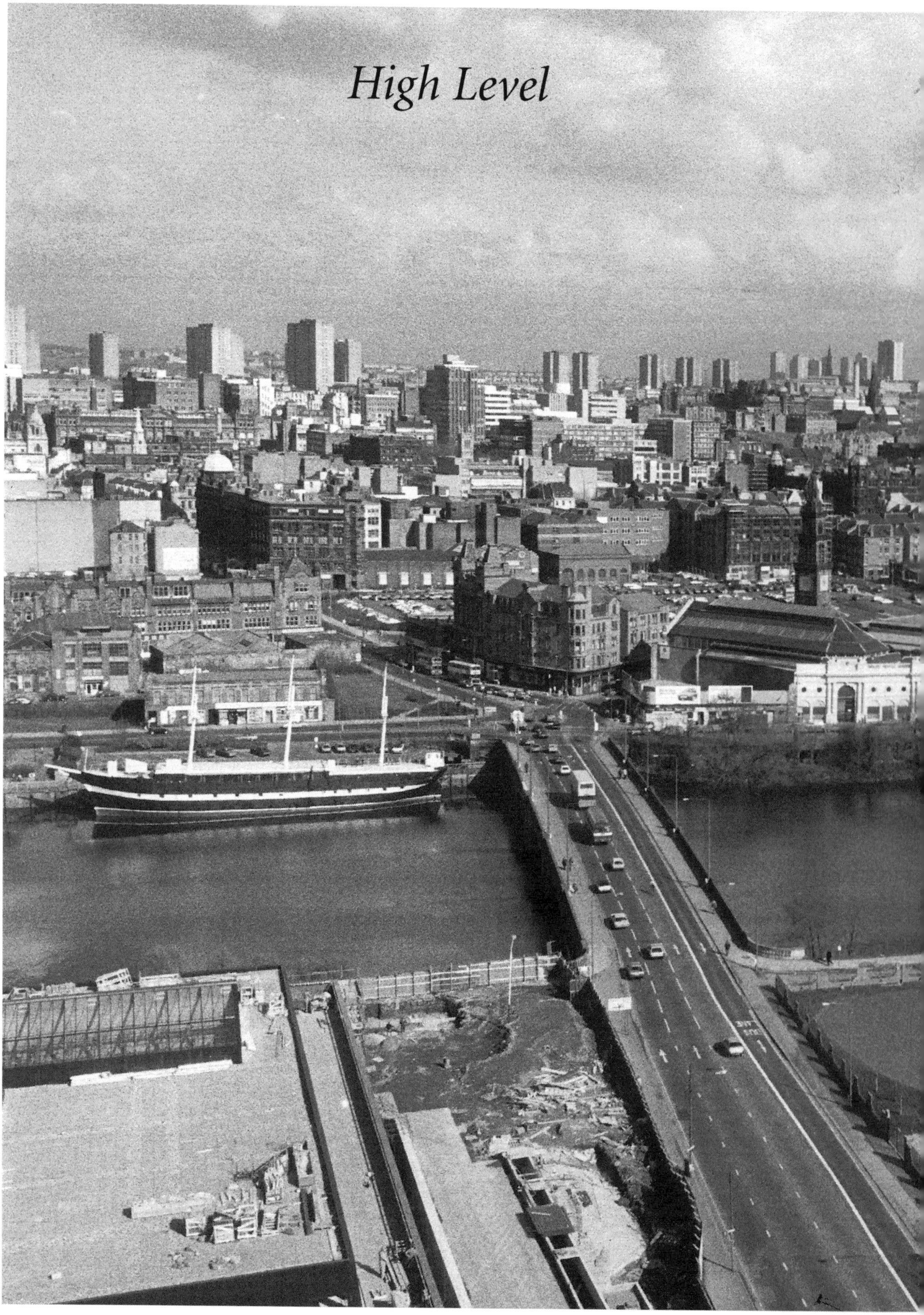

The view from one of the modern Gorbals high flats with the sailing vessel *Carrick* moored on the Clyde. The new Sheriff Court is under construction on the left and the City Mosque is on the right. The *Carrick*, formerly the *City of Adelaide*, was moved to the Scottish Maritime Museum in Irvine in 1992.   *1-01.*

A 1960s view of an area now dominated by the Concert Hall. Both the old Buchanan Street passenger and freight railway terminals are visible as is Buchanan Street bus station. *I-03*

An aerial view of Queen's Dock, probably the early 1960s. The Dock opened in 1877 and closed in 1969 when it was filled in and in 1985 became the site of the Scottish Exhibition and Conference Centre, a controversial structure known to Glaswegians as the 'Big Red Shed'. Some of the infill came from the old St Enoch railway station.   *I-04*

Knightswood was the site of Glasgow's biggest inter-war housing project with 10,000 homes completed by March 1935. Here's how it looked from the air in the 1950s. This low density housing contrasted starkly with the post-war schemes like Castlemilk and Drumchapel.   *1-05*

A spectacular view across the city taken during the construction of multi-storey flats in Castlemilk in 1962.   *1-06*

A high level city centre view with the College of Building and Printing under construction in 1962 and the City Chambers. *1-07*

An aerial view of Ravenscraig before nationalisation when the steel works were still part of Colvilles.   *I-08*

An impressive aerial view showing the size of the Empire Exhibition in Bellahouston Park in 1938 with the old White City Stadium – home of speedway and dog racing – off Paisley Road West visible in the background.   *I-09*

An unusual view of the Kelvin Hall taken from the University in 1950 when there was still commercial shipping coming up into the heart of Glasgow. *I-10*

A 1960s shot of St Enoch Railway Station, St Enoch Hotel and St Enoch Square with Lewis's department store prominent on the left and Arnott Simpsons store under construction. Note the cranes on the river bank, which is now a pedestrian walkway. *I-11*

Milngavie from the air in the late 1960s showing the northern extremity of the Glasgow conurbation. Top right is Mugdock Reservoir, part of the Loch Katrine water scheme.   *1-12*

The old tenements of Ballater Street and Rutherglen Road in the Gorbals have fallen to the bulldozers leaving gaps to be filled by new housing in Waddell Court and Queen Elizabeth Square in this 1960s aerial shot.   *1-13*

Street Level

The oldest building in Glasgow, Provand's Lordship, built around 1471, was refurbished in the 1990s but here is how it looked in 1956. Note the woman, complete with a steamie load of washing on a bogie. *I-14*

The corner of Argyle Street and Union Street showing the Adelphi Hotel, now demolished. *I-15*

Glasgow Cross around 1912 showing the equestrian statue of King William of Orange and the Tontine buildings. The statue was moved in 1923 to Cathedral Square. The tail, on a ball and socket joint, is supposed to move in the wind. *I-16*

Blythswood Square had a slightly unsavoury night-time reputation but during the day it is a popular place for office workers to take the sun. This was how it looked in August 1956. *I-17*

The Battlefield Rest outside the Victoria Infirmary has been a southside landmark for many years. Now restored and converted to an Italian restaurant, here it is in the 1950s on a dreich November day. *I-18*

An unusual 1962 view of the Cathedral looking down Wishart Street from Alexandra Parade. *I-19*

Rolland Street, Maryhill, in May 1953 – a mass of flags and bunting to celebrate the forthcoming Coronation of Queen Elizabeth. *I-20*

The junction of Queen Street and Ingram Street in January 1956 before the British Linen Bank building was replaced by an unattractive modern block. *I-21*

The flavour of the West End in the 1930s in this view at Kelvinside Church and the Botanic Gardens and Great Western Road. The pavement had just been widened without losing the trees. *I-22*

Buckingham Terrace, one of several fine terraces off Great Western Road, on a dull day in March 1957.   *1-23*

Wide and handsome…looking west from Byres Road along Great Western Road, much praised architecturally, in the early 1970s.   *1-24*

Anniesland Cross in 1963 during one of its many reconstructions with the last of the tramrails being removed and a prefab still proudly presiding over the scene.   *1-25*

The imposing sweep of Park Circus is blighted with parked cars in this 1990 view.   *1-26*

The early 1970s saw a change in policy away from demolition in favour of rehabilitation of Glasgow's characteristic tenements. Here an impressive restoration job has been done on south-side flats at Queen's Drive facing the greenery of Queen's Park.   *1-27*

South Portland Street: A typical bleak example of the Gorbals streetscape before the bulldozers altered its appearance for ever.   *I-28*

The great gale of January 1968 which caused millions of pounds worth of damage prompted some demolition but also much restoration and a general cleaning up of the city's magnificent Victorian architecture. Here's how Preston Street, Govanhill, looked on the morning after the great blow.   *I-29*

Paisley Road West looking west near Lorne Street in the late 1950s.   *1-30*

Corner of Cowcaddens Street and Stow Street looking towards Queen's Arcade in the mid 1950s.   *1-31*

A 1976 view of Paisley Road Toll, the site of the original toll booth for traffic between Glasgow and Paisley.   *I-32*

The junction of Argyle Street and Oswald Street and Hope Street on a snowy January day in the mid 1950s.   *I-33*

One of the archive's final pictures of the old Gorbals around the 1960s.   *1-34*

Gorbals Cross as it looked in the 1930s before the demolition of the fountain.   *1-35*

Gorbals Cross in the late 1940s, unrecognisable from its appearance today.   *1-36*

Charing Cross in 1956 with the Grand Hotel towering over the trams.   *1-37*

Glasgow Cross in 1946 showing the Tolbooth Steeple about to become an island in the middle of the traffic.   *1-38*

The Uddingston tram heads out through Parkhead Cross early in the 20th century. *1-39*

Main Street, Rutherglen in the mid 1950s. Wide and spacious with most of the shops protecting their windows with the obligatory sun shades of the era. At this stage trams no longer ran in the Main Street. *1-40*

Rutherglen Main Street again, this time in 1926 when the Burgh was celebrating the eighth centenary of its Royal charter. Cloche hats, stately prams and a lone tram add to the period atmosphere.   *1-41*

A telephoto shot of the south-side hub – Victoria Road – pulls the city centre much closer to the Queen's Park gates than it is in reality. This view was taken in March 1991.   *1-42*

Shawls were still something of a fashion statement in this 1933 picture of crowds cheering the Prince of Wales during a visit to Main Street, Bridgeton.   *1-43*

A very early picture of New Apothecaries Hall in Glassford Street at the junction of Wilson Street.   *1-44*

Behind the grim walls lies Duke Street prison as it was before it was demolished and replaced by high-rise housing.   *1-45*

The Queen and the Duke of Edinburgh pass outside the old *Herald* and *Evening Times* offices in Buchanan Street in 1953 long before Buchanan Street became a pedestrian precinct.   *1-46*

The regeneration of the Merchant City in the 1980s produced some attractive new buildings and some remarkable transformations. The centrepiece of this shot is the old Campbell, Stewart and MacDonald's warehouse in Ingram Street which became the Houndsditch Building before being converted into flats.   *1-47*

New flats in the Merchant City which were awarded the Medal of Honour in the Europa Nostra 1988 Annual Awards.
1-48

This thatched cottage on the road to Cathkin Braes was the birthplace of James Gilmour, a missionary in Mongolia. A plaque on the wall told his story.   *1-49*

The 18th fairway of Linn Park, one of Glasgow's 18-hole municipal courses, on a sunny day in September 1957. Castlemilk housing looms in the background as industrial units are under construction. The houses on the hillside were renovated in the mid 1990s.   *1-50*

Fresh paint and a new design look help renew Castlemilk, one of Glasgow's largest peripheral schemes, in the 1990s.
I-51

The smiling face of the renovation of Castlemilk. Fifteen-year-old Nicola Davidson designed this logo as part of the Castlemilk Partnership's moves to regenerate the scheme. Here she is congratulated by Tiger Tim Stevens, the DJ who made his name with Radio Clyde.   *I-52*

This was Easter Sunday down on the farm in 1949 with the 16th century Peel of Drumry standing surrounded by cows, hens and horses. It was controversially demolished in the late 1950s.   *I-53*

The same scene in the 1950s after the building of the Drumchapel housing scheme.   *I-54*

Street theatre in the early 1900s. City children watch a Punch and Judy show at the corner of Rose Street and Sauchiehall Street.   *I-55*

Cuthbertson's was one of the most famous music shops in the city, pictured here in 1964. It stood on the site of a country house originally owned by wealthy Glasgow merchants in the 18th century. The foundations of the old house could still be seen in the basement of the building which also contained a well, thought to have been in the garden at the back of the original house.   *I-56*

An imposing home for pianos, organs and 'complete house furnishings' …Woodley's was at the junction of College Street and High Street.   *1-57*

Turn of the century shot of Thomson's who sold pianos and organs. The staff stand proudly at the front door. According to the caption this was a time of rapid expansion for Govan Road.   *1-58*

Two faces of Glasgow housing are
shown in this 1986 shot of
Hogganfield Street in Blackhill.   *I-59*

A home in Aros Drive,
Mosspark, is a typical
example of the garden
suburb type of house built in
the inter-war years. A door
of your own and bit of
garden for everyone.   *I-60*

Clarkston Road, Muirend, in the
1970s looking towards the Safeway
Supermarket and the Toledo Cinema.
This is right on the border between
Glasgow and Renfrewshire.   *I-61*

A tranquil scene in Milngavie, Glasgow's equivalent of the stockbroker belt, with a view of Tannoch Loch.   *I-62*

The old Shaw Bridge over the River Cart at Pollokshaws was built in 1654 but demolished in the mid 1930s.   *I-63*

A City with Style

Scotland Street School, built 1904 – 1906, a fine example of Charles Rennie Mackintosh's work. It is now Scotland Street School Museum.   *1-64*

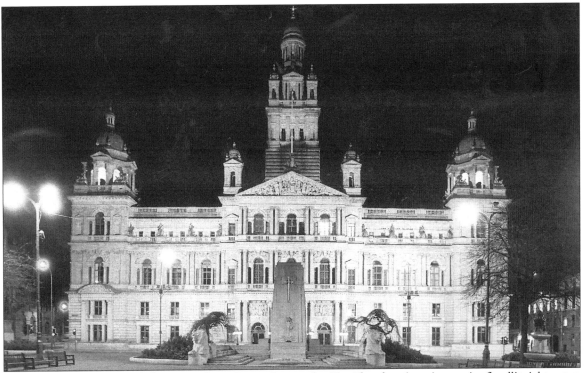

Late at night with the crowds long gone from George Square, the City Chambers is an impressive floodlit sight.   *1-65*

Fifty teenagers from Berlin and Strathclyde reunite in 1990 for a City of Culture dance sequence, choreographed by Royston Maldoom to Stravinsky's *Music for the Rite of Spring*, which had created a sensation at a youth festival in Berlin the previous summer as part of an exchange between the past and future cultural capitals of Europe.   *I-68*

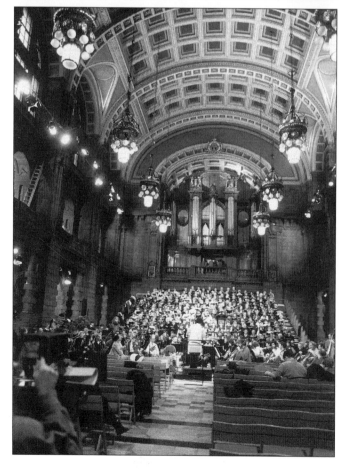

Choirs fill the magnificence of the interior of the Kelvingrove Art Gallery & Museum with sound as part of Glasgow's celebration as the European City of Culture 1990.   *I-67*

The massive Finnieston crane is one of the Clyde's oldest and biggest. In the mid 1980s it was floodlit to provide some Christmas sparkle for the riverside.   *I-66*

Frank Sinatra was one of the stars of the
Year of Culture. His LA publicist asked the
Evening Times for a copy of this picture
taken at Ibrox for 'Mr. Sinatra's personal use'.
Happy to oblige.
I-69

One of the most memorable sights and
sounds of the Garden Festival was the Coca-
Cola ride, the screams from which could be
heard right across the river and into the
town. Here in 1988, huge queues of people
are willing to sample the noisy thrill of a
lifetime.   *I-70*

The opening day of the Festival was an unforgettable Glasgow occasion. Here Princess Diana, Prince Charles and Scottish Secretary Malcolm Rifkind share the open-top deck of an old city tram as crowds throng the festival site and boats crowd the river.   *I-71*

The striking exterior of the former Beresford Hotel in Sauchiehall Street seen in 1952 before a change of use to the Baird Hall of Residence for Strathclyde University students. Built for the 1938 Empire Exhibition it was for a time the tallest building in Glasgow.   *I-72*

Putting on the style – this was how a city centre watering hole looked in 1938 as the cocktail barman in the Beresford drops a little something uplifting into the chrome cocktail shaker. *I-73*

The *Glasgow Herald* pavilion at the Empire Exhibition in Bellahouston Park in 1938. The exhibition ran from May to October and attracted around 12 million, less than the 20 million anticipated – largely put down to a wet and windy summer! *I-74*

Tait's Tower is a striking spectacle against the Bellahouston Park night sky at the Empire Exhibition. Its Sunday name was the Tower of Empire. Thomas Smith Tait was the architect-in-chief for the exhibition.
1-75

A bleak winter scene – looking into Royal Exchange Square off Buchanan Street in the late 1940s.
1-76

The Glasgow skyline with the famous Greek Thomson Church in Caledonia Road in the foreground taken from Gushetfaulds container depot in 1970.   *1-77*

The grim splendour of the Necropolis towers over the smog and gloom of the city centre in 1966.   *1-79*

St Andrew's Parish Church in St Andrew's Square in its heyday. In the 1990s it is being restored as a centrepiece to a new housing development. *1-78*

In from the cold – a Sunday afternoon in the Kelvingrove Art Gallery & Museum in the 1930s was a favourite way for citizens to spend an hour or two enjoying the splendid collection of works of art.   *I-80*

Still a popular way to beat the weather. Here in the 1990s two toddlers take off their wellies before a spot of serious wildlife exploration.   *I-81*

Glasgow businessmen enjoy a coffee in Cooper's Tearooms in Ingram Street which were formerly Miss Cranston's. The tearooms were bought by Glasgow Corporation in the 1950s to preserve the premises as an example of the work of Charles Rennie Mackintosh but were dismantled in 1971. *1-84*

A dramatic exterior of Charles Rennie Mackintosh's much acclaimed Glasgow School of Art, acknowledged worldwide as a successful blend of Arts and Crafts and Art Nouveau ideals. It was built between 1898 and 1906. *1-82*

Interior details
of the Charles
Rennie
Mackintosh
library inside
the School of
Art in Renfrew
Street. *1-83*

Craig's smokeroom and picture gallery in the basement of the Gordon Street restaurant as it was on the last day of business, Saturday, 2 April 1955.   *I-85*

Inside Samuel Dow's Pub in Mitchell Street next door to the old *Herald* and *Evening Times* building and a much frequented haunt of the newspaper workers, a fact underlined by the décor.   *I-86*

Miss Cranston was an enthusiastic patron of the young Charles Rennie Mackintosh who was involved in the design of several of her tea rooms, including this one at the corner of Argyle Street and Queen Street.   *I-87*

Shipping magnate Sir William Burrell in 1944 bequeathed his magnificent and eclectic art collection to the City of Glasgow on condition that a building to house it be built not less than 16 miles from the city centre. With the abatement of pollution the Trustees agreed to a site in Pollok Park, a 'rural' location within the city. The Gallery was opened by the Queen in 1983.   *I-88*

Inside the Burrell – live music amid the bright acres of spaces of the gallery as the Scottish Chamber Orchestra entertains on an autumn day in 1987. *I-89*

Pollok House, built between 1748 and 1752 as the family home of the Maxwells of Pollok, seen here in the 1970s looking just as it must have done when built. *I-90*

A 1980s shot showing the colourful mosaics and marbled splendour just inside the main entrance to the City Chambers.
I-91

Templeton's carpet factory in Glasgow Green was built after the style of the Doge's Palace in Venice because John Templeton believed that factories could be places of beauty, not just for the workers but for the sake of the arts. In 1889, before completion of the whole structure, a wall collapsed killing 30 women workers in the weaving sheds. In 1900 a fire killed another 70 people on the site.   *I-92*

The Rogano is one of the city's most famous Art Deco restaurants. After a period of decline it was restored in the 1980s to its original 1930s glory. The impressive figure is doorman Alfred Pickles, pictured here in 1985. *I-93*

Open-top trams pass the Kelvin Hall, rebuilt in 1927 after a fire in 1925. *I-94*

Kelvin Court luxury flats off Great Western Road under construction in 1939. The notice board advertises central heating, constant hot water, ten electric lifts, built-in furniture, labour saving devices, refrigerators, tiled kitchens, glass bathrooms and liveried porters.   *I-95*

An unusual view of the turrets of the Royal Infirmary taken around the 1970s.   *I-96*

Having Fun

Doon the watter …the paddle steamer *Glen Rosa* takes Fair Holiday crowds across the Firth to Rothesay in 1937.
I-97

One of the most popular attractions on the steamers that sailed 'doon the watter' was always the band. Here they get ready to entertain the passengers on a crowded *King Edward* leaving the Broomielaw to head down the river during Glasgow Fair 1939. *I-98*

The *King Edward* again, this time moored at Rothesay Pier in the late 1940s.   *I-99*

A trip 'doon the watter' usually began with a rail journey and here a family set out for a Fair Holiday break in July 1915 with the man of the house showing some unusual skill with a case and his wife looking none too happy at the change of sink.   *I-100*

Another July ritual. Passengers queue at Broomielaw to board the *Royal Ulsterman* bound for Belfast in 1960.   *I-101*

"Hurry, hurry, we'll miss the train," seems to be the cry as a father heads for the coast with natty sports jacket and golf clubs, something of a contrast to the battered suitcase and pram.   *I-102*

Maw, Paw and the weans. This time heading into the old St Enoch Station on a summer day some time in the 1950s.
I-103

Glasgow's Buchanan Street Station had a narrow, sloping concourse unsuited to crowds so it is fortunate that scenes such as this, from July 1954, were largely restricted to summer holiday demand. A typical day tended to have flurries of activity followed by long periods of hiatus; more like a country terminus than a main city station. Note the English-style helmet of the British Transport Commission policeman.   *I-104*

The most distinctive feature of Glasgow Central was its departure indicator. Housed in a torpedo-shaped building, it relied on manually-positioned screens and survived until 1985. This picture dates from 1963. It is the Glasgow Fair and the weather, judging by the clothes, is not untypical! *I-105*

Glasgow Central Station, when rebuilt in 1901-06, was designed for crowds, with platform ends staggered in front of a slightly sloping concourse and an emphasis on curved building lines and rounded corners. The theory was that surging throngs of people, like flowing water, find the line of least resistance. There was also insufficient space to accommodate queues of would-be holiday travellers, like this 1938 horde. *I-106*

St Enoch (or St Enoch's as it was popularly known) was quite the gloomiest of Glasgow's four main stations; a trifle incongruous as it was the first major public building in the city to be lit by electricity. It also had a distinctive aroma created by whisky stored in its underground vaults and the pigeons which plagued its roof. After closure in June 1966 it was used as a car park for a few ignominious years.　*I-107*

Crowds no longer throng Glasgow's major railway stations as citizens head for the Clyde coast …the congestion has moved with the times as this 1987 shot of holiday-makers waiting at Glasgow Airport for jets to the sun shows. *I-108*

The world's last surviving sea-going paddle steamer, the *Waverley*, and the Renfrew Ferry seen in 1993. The ferry has been converted and moved up river to become a popular venue for ceilidhs and concerts. *I-109*

All the fun of the fair at Glasgow Fair. This was Glasgow Green in July 1946 as families began to enjoy the post-war era. *I-110*

Third Lanark Football Club, which used to play at Cathkin Park, no longer exists. Here a Hi-Hi stalwart, Hugh Smith, tends his kiddies' roundabout at the Glasgow Green Fair in 1956.   *I-111*

Students' Charities Day was a great Glasgow institution. In 1933 the procession leaves Gilmorehill with the fancy dressed students ready to rattle their cans to raise cash.   *I-112*

Govan Fair in June always attracted huge crowds. The 1958 procession passes Govan Cross led by the Glasgow Police Pipe Band followed by the Royal Navy Volunteer Reserve band. *I-113*

The Boys' Brigade wasn't all polishing boots and belts and smartly turned out kit. Eager anticipation on the faces of city boys shines out as, kitbags on their shoulders, a Glasgow company bound up the approaches to St Enoch station heading for summer camp at Ballantrae. *I-114*

Like the Scouts the Boys' Brigade – founded in Glasgow by William Smith in 1883 – were a vital part of local life. Here Admiral of the Fleet Lord Beatty, Col. W.D.Scott, Lord Provost John Stewart and Lord Blythswood inspect a parade in the Queen's Park recreation ground.   *I-115*

The Scout Gang Shows were a winter tradition for many years. The young people who starred in an item called Mexico are pictured backstage in the Theatre Royal in 1939. In later years the city's gang shows were presented in the King's.   *I-116*

Mind the paintwork! Bare feet are the order of the day as Scouts Alan Cook and David Armstrong of the 43rd Glasgow troop give a car a wash and brush up for Bob-a-Job week in the early 1950s. This fund-raising scheme has declined in importance, a victim of a changing social climate. *I-117*

Scouting played an important role for the city's youth down the years and here Scotstoun Showground hears the skirl of the pipes as a group of Rover Scouts go on parade in 1929. *I-118*

Rouken Glen and a trip round the island in the motor boat has long been a south-side attraction. Here in 1939 the skipper looks well enough dressed to captain the *QE2* while the youngsters enjoy themselves as he weaves round the rowing boats.   *I-119*

The city's great and the good enjoyed rowing boats as much as the ordinary citizenry. Here are some of the official party at the opening of Hogganfield Loch on 4 July 1924.   *I-120*

West End rowers enjoy a jaunt on a summer's day in Bingham's Pond off Great Western Road. This scene has St John's Renfield Church prominent in the background.   *I-121*

Men and boys crowd on to the good ship *Bumbee* but it appears that Ma and wee Jeanie prefer to stay ashore according to the original caption of this picture taken at Burnside Loch, Rutherglen around 1915. The Burnside boating pond has long since vanished from the suburban scene.   *I-122*

This view of the St Andrew's Suspension Bridge shows a boat hiring station on the left and the People's Palace, the Cathedral and the Royal Infirmary in a smoky background.   *I-123*

Fountains can be practical as well as beautiful. Here youngsters cool off in the Stewart Memorial Fountain in Kelvingrove Park during a long hot summer with an imposing view of the University in the background. The fountain was erected in honour of Lord Provost Robert Stewart of Murdostoun in recognition of his role in commissioning the Loch Katrine water supply for the city.   *I-124*

Glasgow University and the audience watching the park entertainers in Kelvingrove are reflected in the River Kelvin during a heatwave in July 1948.   *I-125*

Poised for action… swimmers ready for the big plunge in the relay race during Glasgow Schools Swimming Association's annual gala at Govanhill Baths in Calder Street in October 1955.   *I-126*

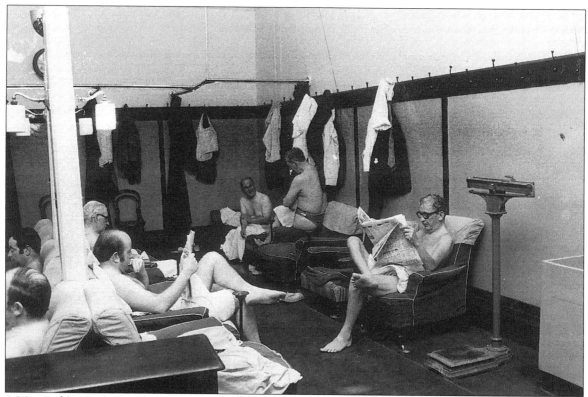

A West End institution – Arlington Baths. Here in the 1970s Glasgow businessmen relax before taking exercise to fight the flab. *I-127*

A mum and toddler go for a stroll in Kelvingrove Park with Woodlands Terrace and Park Gardens in the background of this 1952 shot. *I-128*

One of the most popular attractions at Calderpark Zoo. Youngsters queue to get a ride on an elephant in August 1948. *I-129*

Elephants' antics in the old Kelvin Hall Circus arena in 1949. *I-130*

The country comes to town – this was the annual stallion show held at Scotstoun Showground in 1959, its 99th year. This was the judging for the best filly, two-year-olds and over.   *I-131*

George Square, always at the centre of great events in city life, also has a more relaxing side. Here citizens take the sun in the 1950s as they have done summer after summer.   *I-132*

On the Town

For the gent, the raincoat over the arm, for the lady, a coat draped casually over the shoulders. A taxi stands at the ready… dancers leave the Dennistoun Palais de Danse in the late 1950s.   *I-133*

Another Glasgow ballroom favourite was the Locarno in Sauchiehall Street shown here probably in the late fifties. The Locarno was much favoured by US servicemen during the war.   *I-134*

An appreciative audience watches the skill and grace of contestants in the Scottish Dancing Championships at The Albert in 1957 when there was a huge interest in competitive dancing.
I-135

Dreich Glasgow streets: glittering Glasgow nights… since its rebirth in the early 1980s, Barrowland has hosted gigs by some of the world's top rock acts from David Bowie to U2.
I-136

Timeless two-step… Hogmanay 1982, and Barrowland Ballroom *aficionados* echo the foxtrotting 1940s. George McGowan leads the band.   *1-137*

Glasgow has a great reputation as a dancing-daft city and for many couples a night at the dancing meant only one place – The Albert Ballroom in Bath Street.
1-138

Hollywood glitter in Glasgow as The Paramount in Renfield Street, now the Odeon, is floodlit on a cold January night in 1935. *I-139*

The Coliseum Picture House in Eglinton Street – now a bingo hall – is mobbed for the 1931 Charlie Chaplin hit *City Lights*. *I-140*

Harry Lauder opened the imposing new Embassy cinema in Shawlands.   *1-141*

Believed to have been one of the oldest continuously operated cinemas in Britain, the Salon in Hillhead was controversially closed in October 1992 when the owners removed the seats. The future of this B-listed building remains in doubt after the failure of plans for conversion to a sports hall or a 'multi-media cinema/dining experience'.   *1-142*

One of Glasgow's earliest
cinemas rejoiced in the title of
the Eglinton Electreum. This is
it in its final days.   *I-144*

1930s housing estates like King's
Park tended to have a popular
local cinema. Here is the State in
King's Park with dramatic white
walls and a touch of Art Deco
standing out against the night sky
and its suburban surroundings.
I-145

The Elephant Cinema in Shawlands built by the eccentric millionaire A.E.Pickard in the 1930s and originally called the White Elephant closed down in the 1960s. *1-146*

Variety star Dave Willis surrounded by showgirls at the opening night of the Theatre Royal panto in 1939. *1-147*

Lex McLean attracted huge audiences to his Pavilion Theatre show for a succession of seasons from the mid 1950s. Also on many of the bills were the famous May Moxon Young Ladies. Here Lex entertains them. Lex could play to 18,000 people a week.
I-148

Rikki Fulton as Francie and Jack Milroy as Josie, two comic, gallus, Glasgow characters, developed a huge following in the 1960s. Despite their success the partnership split with Rikki building himself an impressive career as a straight actor and Jack continuing in comedy but public demand brought them together on many occasions after the official end of the partnership.
I-149

Matt McGinn of the Calton (1928-77) was a song writer who played an important part in the folk and protest movements in the 1960s and 1970s. He also worked as an actor. Here he is as Sammy McGuigan, a bus driver, in STV's *High Living*, a drama series about life in high-rise flats.   *I-150*

With the gangliness of a big 'daft laddie', and the sleekit cunning of a disingenuous rogue, Duncan Macrae (1905-67) was the great comic genius of the Scottish stage, as comfortable with Chekhov or Shakespeare as he was with variety or pantomime. He gave Scottish acting a distinctive flair. Here (pictured left) he plays the bewitched Donald to James Gibson's Dugald in a 1944 premiere of James Bridie's *The Forrigan Reel*, by the Citizens' Theatre at its first home in the Athenaeum.   *I-151*

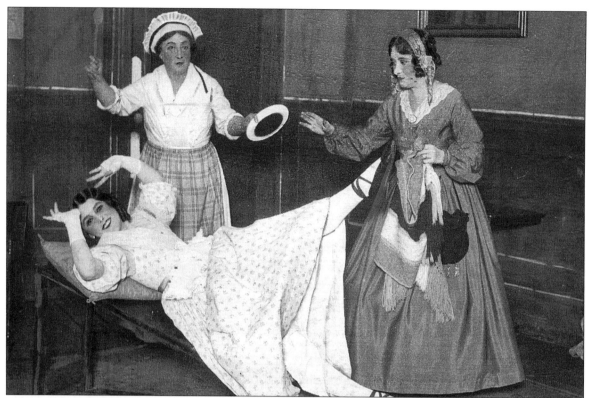

The Scottish comedy *Marigold* was produced by the Glasgow Repertory Company at the Theatre Royal in 1927. Rubina Macfarraline played the title role.   *I-152*

A motley crew – the cast of *Robinson Crusoe* at the King's in 1974 take to the Clyde in a piratical publicity stunt. Larry Marshall, of STV's *One O'Clock Gang,* and Rikki Fulton are in the forefront. Others in the picture include Walter Carr, Una McLean and Pat Lancaster.   *I-153*

In the 1960s the BBC's White Heather Club was one of the most popular TV shows. Andy Stewart and Robert Wilson are seen taking part in the 160th edition. *1-154*

Bertha Waddell and her Children's Theatre was an institution in the 1950s, appearing before primary kids in such venues as the Couper Institute in Cathcart. Here, with Geoffrey Waddell as a clown, she appears in the Co-operative Hall in Springburn.   *1-155*

James Bridie (1888-1951) was the founding father of the Citizens' Theatre. His real name was Dr Osborne Henry Mavor, writer, general practitioner and consultant, and he gave the company a prescription of health that would see it through its first half century. He is pictured (third from the left) on 11 September 1945, opening night for the Citizens' moving to its present home in the former Royal Princess Theatre in Gorbals. The production was J.B.Priestley's *Johnson Over Jordan.*   *I-156*

From 1969 under the artistic directorship of Giles Havergal, the company broadened its citizenship, with an international reputation and solid community support, encouraged by an egalitarianism in uniform seat prices (held at 90p into the 1980s, OAPs and unemployed free) and exciting theatricality. Havergal celebrated 25 years at the Citizens' with the City of Glasgow's most prestigious award, the St Mungo Prize, in 1995.   *I-157*

MAYFEST present 3–21 MAY
THE TRAVERSE
THEATRE COMPANY IN
PAISLEY PATTERNS
THE SLAB BOYS . STILL LIFE .
CUTTIN A RUG
Written and Designed by John Byrne
Directed by David Hayman

WITH IAIN ANDREW. FREDDIE BOARDLEY. ANDREW GRAY
ELAINE COLLINS. GERARD KELLY, ALEXANDER MORTON
NICHOLAS SHERRY

DAVID HAYMAN as Phil McCann

Mon. 2	730	*THE SLAB BOYS*
Tue. 3	730	*THE SLAB BOYS*
Wed. 4	730	*CUTTIN A RUG*
Thu. 5	730	*STILL LIFE*
Frid. 6	730	*THE SLAB BOYS*
Sat. 7	1200	*THE SLAB BOYS*
	400	*CUTTIN A RUG*
	800	*STILL LIFE*
Mon. 9	730	*STILL LIFE*
Tue. 10	730	*THE SLAB BOYS*
Wed. 11	730	*CUTTIN A RUG*
	730	*STILL LIFE*
		THE SLAB BOYS

p FREE Public Dress Rehearsal

Mon. 16		*THE SLAB BOYS*
Tue. 17		*THE SLAB BOYS*
Wed. 18		*CUTTIN A RUG*
Thu. 19		*STILL LIFE*
Frid. 20		*THE SLAB BOYS*
Sat. 21	1200	*THE SLAB BOYS*
	400	*CUTTIN A RUG*
	800	*STILL LIFE*

£2
£1

OAPs AND UNEMPLOYED FREE

Freewheeling to the Citizens', Bridgeton boy David Hayman was one of the protégés of the first decade of the Havergal regime, and he has gone up through the gears to a distinguished career as actor and director in television, film and stage. Here he arrives at the theatre for the John Byrne Paisley Patterns trilogy, which he directed for the Traverse Theatre Company, Edinburgh, for the first Glasgow Mayfest in 1983. *1-158*

The Citizens', originally the Royal Princess Theatre, changed its name in 1945. The Doric column façade was removed in 1978 but the statues on the skyline were saved to star permanently in the new foyer. *1-159*

The Citizens' Theatre in the Gorbals took on a modernistic look in the 1990s. Some of the sculptures that used to grace the old façade can be glimpsed through the glass. *I-160*

Glasgow's claim to the title 'European City of Culture' was reinforced when it staged the only UK performances of Peter Brook's Indian epic, *The Mahabharata*, in 1988. Brook brought his internationally acclaimed theatre company, CICT, to the city because the Council converted a south side tram depot specifically to accommodate the demanding requirements of the production. The legacy is The Tramway, now an integral part of Glasgow's cultural life. *I-161*

The new Glasgow Concert Hall was opened in time for the Year of Culture in 1990. Its exterior attracted much criticism but there was general praise for the striking interior – its bars, open gathering places and its remarkable acoustics. Here the Scottish National Orchestra rehearse for a concert.   *I-162*

In the wait for the new Concert Hall, the Proms had a temporary home in the Kelvin Hall. In 1979 an informally dressed Alexander Gibson entertains the promenaders in style.   *I-163*

After the St Andrew's Halls fire the former Gaiety Theatre at Anderston Cross became the temporary Glasgow Concert Hall and the short-term home of the Scottish National Orchestra. This was how it looked on opening day in January 1963.   *I-164*

Scottish Ballet has earned an enviable reputation over the years. In addition to memorable performances at the Theatre Royal it has taken ballet out and about to small halls and schools. Here the Scottish Ballet Workshop limbers up on the street before heading out on an assignment. The dancers are, left to right, Hilary Clark, Alasdair MacNeill, Susan Cooper, Frank Chin, Chris Blagdon and Rowan Taylor.   *I-165*

The old Scotia Music Hall in Stockwell Street which became the Metropole. It burned down in 1961 and Jimmy Logan took the name to the Empress in St George's Cross. But the Ye Olde Scotia Inn in Stockwell Street is still a haunt of folk musicians and writers.   *I-166*

The Empire in Sauchiehall Street was home to all the big names of variety right up until its demolition in 1963. It gained a fearful reputation among English comedians, many of whom 'died' on Monday night first houses as their humour failed to survive the journey north.   *I-168*

The Alhambra Theatre in Waterloo Street was famous for its glossy Five Past Eight reviews starring, among others, Jack Radcliffe, Jimmy Logan, Stanley Baxter and Max Bygraves. It was demolished in 1971 and its dull and unattractive office block replacement was scheduled to suffer the same fate in the 1990s. *I-167*

The façade of the King's Theatre as it looked in the 1920s. The Wolseley car was used on stage in a show called *Out to Win*.   *I-169*

Joe Loss was a great favourite with dancing-daft Glasgow but he was 'in the mood' for something different when he visited the Garden Festival in June 1990. It was swinging kilts instead of dipping trombones. He rounded off that week with concerts in the Motherwell Civic Theatre and the Plaza.   *I-170*

Larger than life… Billy Connolly towers over the Apollo in its heyday in 1975. Once Green's Playhouse – 'Europe's largest cinema' – it latterly became a renowned concert venue as well as a cinema. *1-171*

Few would disagree with the assessment of the *Herald's* rock music critic that Alex Harvey is Glasgow's one true rock and roll son. Introduced on TV as the 'Alex Harvey Band', he insisted that DJ Tony Blackburn give the band its full name – the 'Sensational Alex Harvey Band'. The stage act truly was sensational: a blend of theatre, powerful rock and laconic humour, drawing on material as diverse as Brel's *Next* and Reed's *Delilah* and his own *Faith Healer*. Tragically, he died of a heart attack in 1982 just before his 47th birthday. *1-172*

This mock-up of puffer *The Maggie* attracted huge crowds to the filming of the 1953 movie of the same name, starring Paul Douglas. In the United States the title was *High and Dry*. The mock-up was necessary because the authorities would not allow the film company to ground a real ship on the Clyde. A real puffer and a dredger are also in view.   *1-173*

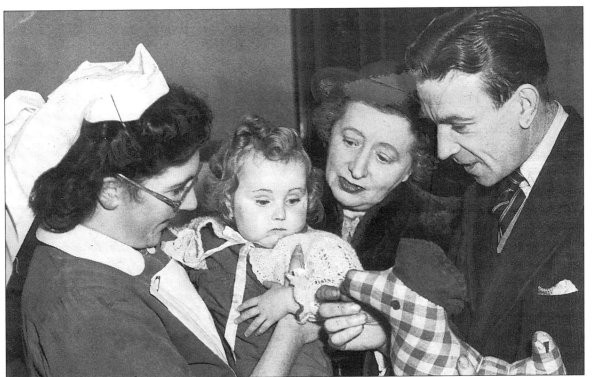

For thousands of children one of the highlights of growing up was *Children's Hour* on BBC Radio. Here in 1947, Willie Joss, famous as Tammy Troot, and Auntie Kathleen, Kathleen Garscadden, visit the Eastpark Home for Children before broadcasting an appeal for funds for the home.   *1-174*

Workshop of the World

The second *Empress of Britain*, launched at Brown's, Clydebank in 1930, described in the original caption as the most beautiful vessel afloat, heading down the Clyde towards the open sea. *I-175*

The third *Empress of Britain* in March 1956 passing down river at Renfrew, taking advantage, as usual, of a high tide. The liner was swept by storms and showers of hail and even had a minor collision on her way from Govan to the Tail of the Bank on a blustery March day in 1956. *I-176*

A historic 1947 picture. The Outram Press mobile wiring van in action for the first time just before it sent this picture back to the *Evening Times*. The liner *Caronia* is seen across the River Clyde in John Brown's shipyard. *1-177*

The measured mile off Arran was the testing place for the great Clyde-built liners. Here the island's peaks form a dramatic back-drop as the *Queen Elizabeth* goes through her paces. *1-178*

The Clyde steamer *Queen Mary 2* which had to be renamed to allow Cunard to use her name for the first of the great Queens, sails around the *Queen Elizabeth* as she lies at the Tail of the Bank.   *I-179*

Britain's last battleship *HMS Vanguard*, built at John Brown's in Clydebank. She was launched on 30 November 1944 – too late to fire a shot in anger. The original *Queen Elizabeth*, being repainted after war service, is in the background. *I-180*

Unfinished but still beautiful – the *QE2* looms large over the Clyde during construction in 1967. Inset: as she looked on a visit to the Clyde in 1994. *I-181*

The Duke of Edinburgh with Sir Eric Yarrow on his right and the Lord Provost of Glasgow Sir Peter Meldrum on his left at the centenary banquet of Yarrow and Co, Scotstoun, in May 1965. Also in the front row (left to right) are Lord Strathclyde, Lady Strathclyde, Lady Yarrow, Lady Meldrum, Mrs William Ross and Willie Ross, Secretary of State for Scotland. *I-182*

The *Cameronia* in Elderslie dry dock where she was converted to an immigrant ship in 1949.   *I-183*

Shipyard workers at Alexander Stephen of Linthouse leaving during a strike in 1957.   *I-184*

Clydeside dockers enjoy a tea break round a brazier in the 1950s. In cold weather the 'pieces' were heated on a toaster made from welding wire.   *1-185*

A splendid 1966 view of Fairfield's Govan yard taken from the crane at the fitting out basin. Craneman Bob Young enjoys a pipe and his daily view.   *1-186*

Glowing forgings roll out from the heat treatment furnace at William Beardmore's Parkhead Works around the 1970s. After the furnace was heated to a temperature of 850 degrees centigrade the forgings were taken to an oil quenching bath as part of the hardening process.   *I-187*

A 50-ton steel casting made at Beardmore's Parkhead Forge arrives at Finnieston Quay in 1938 for shipment to Belfast. It was part of the stern frame for a ship being built at Harland and Wolff's.   *I-188*

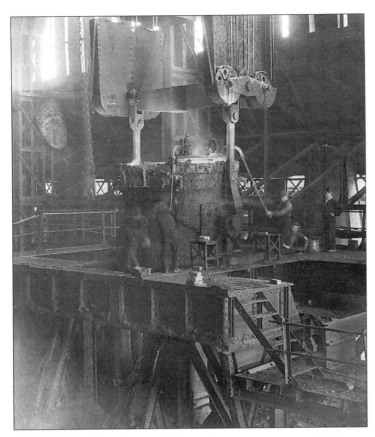

Heat, dirt, danger, massive machinery dwarfing workers – this was how steelworks looked in the early days of production in the west of Scotland. *I-189*

Wartime censorship has obscured the exact location of this picture. The original caption reads: 'Sunday working during the Second World War at a Scottish ordnance factory'. *I-190*

A south-side legend – Dixon's Blazes in Cathcart Road, now the site of a cash and carry. The glare of the flames from this south-side iron works often created spectacular displays in the night sky. Before its demolition Dixon's had been taken over by Colville's Limited.　*I-191*

The use of a telephoto lens to condense the perspective emphasises the contrast between 1960s multi-storey flats and 1930s steam locomotive. The occasion was an open day held at British Rail Engineering's Glasgow Works in June 1981, to mark the plant's 125th anniversary. Of course, it was better known as St Rollox Works or, to generations of Springburn people, as simply the Caley.　*I-192*

A pair of steam traction engines leave the North British Locomotive Company's Hyde Park Works, in Glasgow's Springburn, with a locomotive bound for the docks and ultimately Egypt. The NBL built 32 of these locomotives, in 1947-48. The once-renowned firm went into receivership in 1962.   *I-193*

Locomotives built at the North British works in Springburn are loaded on to the Ellerman Line's *City of Barcelona* at Stobcross Quay *en route* to Bombay. This particular shipment in March 1933 was of seven locomotives each weighing 125 tons.   *I-194*

Bowler hats mix with cloth caps as crowds gather in Townhead to watch the demolition of Tennant's 'stalk' in 1922. The 455ft-high chimney was built in 1841 by the St Rollox Chemical Works to carry off noxious gases.
I-195

The Clyde Tunnel under construction in 1959 as workers sit in the compression chamber used to enter and leave the tunnel. In the 1990s allegations began to surface that the procedure was inadequate and some workers had suffered bone necrosis as a result.
I-196

Barr and Stroud's early premises and work-force in Ashton Lane off Byres Road, an area now packed with trendy bars and restaurants. The company moved from here in 1904 to a base at Anniesland and in 1993 to ultra modern high tech premises in Linthouse.   *1-197*

No retirement at 60 – this 79-year-old was hard at work winding yarn on to bobbins for insertion into spinning looms in a city factory in 1937.   *1-198*

The Singer sewing machine factory in Clydebank at one stage employed more than 12,000 workers, had its own railway station and its own street. The famous clock, a Clydeside landmark, was said to be the second largest in the world with a minute hand almost 13ft long. It was 226ft high. Here in a very early picture the workers stream out at closing time.   *1-199*

This was the shop floor of the Singer factory after a new one-storey building had been erected to replace the former clock tower. Here workers, women and men, are turning out domestic sewing machines at high volume.   *1-202*

The Hoover factory in Cambuslang in the 1950s. According to the original caption the women are winding coils to be inserted into the motor casings. *1-203*

This picture of the Scottish Co-operative Wholesale Society's front in Govan Road was taken in March 1978 shortly before the building was demolished.
1-204

Workers in Templeton's carpet factory in 1939 put the finishing touch to a carpet for the foyer of the Royal
Philharmonic Hall in Liverpool. Designed by Mrs Pinder-Davies of London it took two months to manufacture.
I-205

The W.D. & H.O.Wills factory in Alexandra Parade was a well-known landmark on the eastern approach to the city
before the opening of the M8. The B-listed building, dating from the 1950s, was closed in 1992 and planning
permission for use as students flats was granted.   *I-206*

A million miles away from the modern newspaper office's blinking computer screens, instant worldwide communications satellites and ISDN lines – this was the old *Herald* caseroom in Mitchell Street around the 1960s. The clink of row upon row of linotype machines, the smell of hot metal and the heat coming back in waves off the white tiled walls was unforgettable. *I-207*

A fine mix of bowler hats, briefcases, flat caps and fur coats – this was the old front hall of Outram's building in Buchanan Street in 1933. *I-208*

Glasgow Stock Exchange in 1959 before sombre suits and old fashioned price boards were replaced by the cut of the Armani two-piece and screens linked to the prices in markets round the world.   *I-209*

The airship R34 in July 1919 made the first double crossing of the Atlantic by an aircraft. Some of the early construction of the airship was done in Beardmore's Dalmuir works but the final assembly was at Inchinnan overlooking the main runway at Abbotsinch airport.   *I-210*

Political Life

One of the most famous pictures in the *Herald* archive: The Red Flag is raised in George Square on 27 January 1919 during the so-called 40 Hours Strike. Manny Shinwell, Harry Hopkins and Willie Gallagher, among others, addressed a demonstration in the Square. The police made no attempt to interfere and eventually the crowd dispersed peacefully. A few days later however there were clashes between strikers and police and the army was brought in.   *I-211*

Strikers overturn a Glasgow bus during the General Strike of 1926. The strike initially involved the coal industry, but spread to nearly every other union. The strike lasted only nine days but the miners stayed out for nearly six months.
I-212

John McLean, one of 'Red Clydeside's' legendary figures, seen here shaking hands with the 1919 strikers. Fellow socialist politician David Kirkwood is on the left.   *I-213*

A soldier snatches a few minutes sleep on the floor of the City Chambers where soldiers were quartered during the 1919 strike ready to be called out in an emergency. Following a battle between strikers and police on 31 January the Riot Act was read and troops ordered to Glasgow. The then Secretary of State for Scotland is reported to have claimed it was not a strike, but a Bolshevist rising!   *I-214*

James Maxton, Independent Labour Party MP for Bridgeton from 1922 until his death in 1946. It was said that his votes were weighed, not counted! Seen here, right, with Councillor Myer Galpern and Baillie Carmichael in 1943.   *I-215*

After the reading of the Riot Act during a 40-Hours Strike rally in 1919, the Government ordered troops to Glasgow. Here a tank moves along the Trongate.   *I-216*

Ramsay MacDonald, Labour's first Prime Minister, visited Glasgow several times. Here he is seen, second left, with (left to right) Lady Roberton, Ishbel Macdonald, Sir Hugh Roberton and Paddy Dollan.   *I-217*

Sir Donald McAllister seems to have a point he wishes to make extremely strongly to Lloyd George who was on a visit to Glasgow University in 1922.   *I-218*

Veterans of the Suffragette movement gathered at a rally in Sauchiehall Street in 1949. Here Miss Janet Barrowman, who did two months hard labour in Holloway Prison in 1912 and Mrs Helen Crawford Anderson, who was also sent to Holloway in 1912 and was jailed twice in Glasgow and once in Perth, remember the days of struggle. *I-219*

Anti-English slogans pepper a Renfield Street barrow in 1961. *I-220*

The May Day procession in Buchanan Street on the way to Glasgow Green in 1942 with the banner of the Amalgamated Union of Shop Assistants, Warehousemen and Clerks in the forefront.   *I-221*

There was high security for Russian Premier Alexei Kosygin when he went walkabout in George Square, Glasgow in 1967. Armed security forces watched the proceedings from the rooftops and CND protesters were out in force as Lord Provost John Johnston showed his guest around.   *I-222*

Labour Prime Minister, Harold Wilson meets the enthusiastic citizens of Balgrayhill in Springburn at the opening of new housing in the area in 1968.   *I-223*

Roy Jenkins, one of the founder members of the Social Democratic Party, won a remarkable by-election battle in Hillhead in 1982. Here Jenkins – now Lord Jenkins of Hillhead – travels by underground *en route* to canvassing in Dumbarton Road.   *I-224*

A press conference in Clydebank during the 1971 Upper Clyde Shipbuilders work-in. Jimmy Reid – on the right – recalls that at one such conference someone arrived with a huge quantity of red roses and announced 'this is from Lenin'. The realisation that the 'Lenin' concerned was John Lennon soon dawned as did a feeling of solidarity when it was revealed that along with the roses had come a cheque for £5,000 from John and Yoko. Others in the picture are Bobbie Dickie, a Convener at Brown's, Jimmy Airlie and Con O'Neill, leaders with Reid of one of the most famous industrial actions in Scotland's history.   *I-225*

Religious Life

Children of the Methodist Central Hall Sunday School in Maryhill on their way to Blackhill Farm by horse and cart in the summer of 1965.   *I-226*

They are the unsung heroes of the evangelical movement and you'll find them come Hell or high water, preaching the word each day in Glasgow's Exchange Square. The man with the clarinet is John White, 82 when this picture was taken in 1991, the doyen of the pavement preachers. He describes himself as a simple street salesman – selling God to pedestrians.   *I-227*

Over the years Billy Graham made a remarkable impact on religious life in Glasgow and the West of Scotland. This aerial view shows his Hampden Crusade on 30 April 1955 when 90,000 people thronged the stadium to listen to the world's best known evangelist. *I-228*

American Preacher Billy Graham's charm in action as he meets the Luton Girls Choir on a visit to the City
Chambers in Glasgow in 1954.   *I-229*

In the 1990s the area around the Cathedral was relandscaped and the St Mungo Museum of Religion built in the
precincts. This was how it looked in 1993 with the Royal Infirmary and the Cathedral in the background.   *I-230*

A Requiem Mass in St Andrew's Cathedral in Clyde Street for Pope John XXIII on Friday, 7 June 1963. *I-231*

A meeting of the Workers' Christian Fellowship outside Yarrow's shipyard, Scotstoun in the 1950s. *I-232*

The Kirk always tried to keep in touch with industrial workers. Here the then minister of Partick Parish Church, the Reverend Whitley, shares chat and a mug of tea with local yard workers.   *I-233*

Orange parades attracted massive crowds of spectators in the 1950s. A procession on 11 July 1953 marches down North Frederick Street into George Square.   *I-234*

A sketch from the archives giving a 19th-century view of the Cathedral and the Molendinar Burn. *I-235*

Sporting Heroes

(Left): Every grin tells a story as Billy McNeill leads his pride of Lisbon Lions home in triumph after their momentous 2-1 win over Inter Milan in May 1967, to become the first British club to win the European Cup. Bobby Murdoch, Jimmy Johnstone and Bobby Lennox get in on the act with John Clark sweeping up in the rear.   *1-236*
(Right): Rangers captain John Greig sports a swashbuckling look as he holds the European Cup-winners' trophy aloft after their 3-2 win over Dinamo Moscow in Barcelona in 1972. Derek Johnstone squeezes in on Greig's right with Tommy McLean, Alex MacDonald and Sandy Jardine on the skipper's other flank.   *1-237*

This is the tragic moment which has been woven into the history of Glasgow's twin soccer giants, Rangers and Celtic, the moment Parkhead goalkeeper John Thomson suffered a fatal head injury in September 1931. Thomson, known as the Prince of Goalkeepers, threw himself at the feet of Ibrox centre-forward Sam English and died in hospital. Thousands of mourners walked from Glasgow to his home village of Cardenden in Fife to attend the funeral.   *1-238*

Bowlers, bunnets and trilbies were the order of the day and only one little boy, at the wooden fence, has his head uncovered as the queue wends its way to the turnstiles in this typical Hampden scene in 1926.   *1-239*

Only two more rows to go girls and we're finished. Four Mrs Mopps scrub the seats of Hampden to get the old stadium ready for another onslaught of fans.   *1-240*

Football legislators today would cringe at the sight of this massive crowd packing Hampden in the 1940s with many supporters even sitting on the wall's edge above the entrances as many thousands more patiently waited to get into the old North Stand. The barrowboy on the right must have done a roaring trade.   *I-241*

Pelé's description of 'The Beautiful Game' could have been coined especially for the greatest club match ever played when the maestros of Real Madrid – Puskás, Di Stefano, Gento, etc., – beat Eintracht Frankfurt 7-3 in the European Cup Final at Hampden in 1960. A crowd of 127,000, still a record for a European Cup Final, thrilled by a magnificent display.   *I-242*

Four football legends get together in 1982. Celtic manager Jock Stein, Lisbon Lion Bertie Auld, who also had a spell managing Partick Thistle, Hugh Taylor of the *Evening Times* (perhaps Glasgow's most famous football writer) and John Greig, former captain of Rangers and Scotland. *I-243*

Athletics and five-a-side football… that was the famous Ibrox Sports which marked the end of the athletics season and the start of another Football League campaign. Glasgow journalist Mike Hildrey, then dubbed the 'Balfron Bullet', wins a heat in the 120 yards invitation in 1961. *I-244*

(Left): In the early 1980s attempts were made with the Glasgow Golf Classic to bring big-time golf to Haggs Castle, almost in the city centre. Here two of golf's superstars, Sandy Lyle and Nick Faldo, are ready for action.   *1-245 (Right):* Crossmyloof Ice Rink is long gone, replaced by a supermarket, but this is how it was in its early days with curlers in kilts and plus-fours.   *1-246*

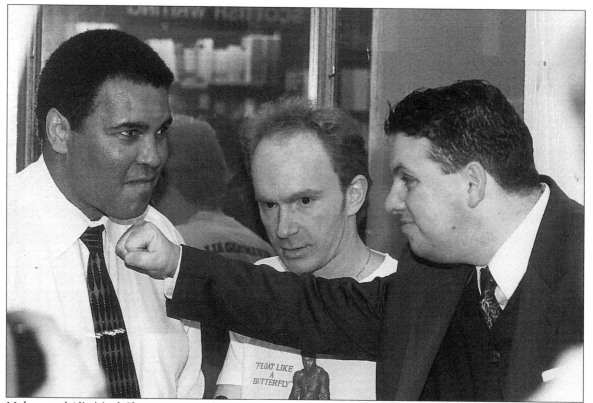

Muhammad Ali visited Glasgow on several occasions during his career. Here he returned in 1993 for a book signing session and took one on the chin with a smile from a Glasgow punter!   *1-247*

Benny Lynch was the trail blazer for Scotland's fighting men, and the first Scot to win a world title. He stopped Jackie Brown in two one-sided rounds and gained universal recognition by outpointing Small Montana, of the Philippines (shown here) in January 1937. Sadly, his decline was rapid and he died in 1946 aged 33, a tragic figure down on his luck.   *1-248*

Joe Gans with his son Walter McGowan as promoter Jack Solomons holds the little Scot's arm high. Walter had just outpointed Italian Salvatore Burruni to win the world flyweight title at Wembley in June 1966. Walter was accompanied by brothers Tommy and David, who acted as seconds.   *1-249*

Peter Keenan (centre) is widely recognised as the finest Scottish boxer *never* to have won a world title. But he won two Lonsdale Belts outright and was also European and Empire bantamweight champion. Perky Peter regularly drew crowds of up to 40,000 to see him fight in the open air in Glasgow football grounds in the 1950s. Peter later turned to promotion and founded the first sporting club in the city which attracted such personalities as film star 'tough guy' Stanley Baker (left) and former unbeaten world heavyweight champion Rocky Marciano who opened the new club.   *I-250*

The Glasgow southpaw Jim Watt after one of his five world title wins in Glasgow. His winning run began with the defeat of Colombian Alfredo Pitalua in April 1979. He lost the title to Alexis Arguello in London in June 1981. 'Cuts man' Dunky Jowett and impresario Jarvis Astaire lead the applause.   *I-251*

Buying and Selling

Either an eye-catching, spectacular piece of modern design or an ugly overgrown glass house. Opinions on the St Enoch Centre vary but no one can deny its dramatic impact on the city centre.   *I-252*

Princes Square was one of the most successful new shopping complexes in the city centre. Up-market shops, restaurants, barrows selling novelty goods and diversions like this fashion display in 1994 make it a mecca for city centre shoppers and visitors.   *I-253*

The entrance to the old Argyll Arcade early in the century. The shops flanking the entrance are Hunter and Company on the left and Stuart Cranston's Tearoom on the right. *1-254*

The brightly lit entrance to the Argyll Arcade as it is now. Close examination of the sign should clear up any doubts regarding the correct spelling of Argyll!   *1-255*

Toy yachts and cars, huge gliders to be created out of patience, balsa wood, tissue paper and banana oil. This was the famous Clyde Model Dock Yard in the Argyll Arcade in the 1960s, a mecca for modellers of all ages.
1-256

Sweets, radios, televisions… shoppers browse out of the rain in Queen's Arcade in 1956. The arcade was demolished in the mid 1960s.   *I-257*

Buchanan Street on a sunny day early at the turn of the century. *I-259*

Umbrellas galore as the rain sweeps down Buchanan Street in 1946.   *1-260*

Spring flower sellers at the bottom of Buchanan Street capitalising on a February day in 1963 when nearly six and a half hours of sunshine made headlines.   *1-261*

Bath Street in the 1950s with Copland and Lye's store prominent. *I-262*

Argyle Street during the Christmas rush in 1951. *I-263*

Springburn Road and the abundance of Co-operative shops shows the dominant part played in the life of Glasgow by the Society. Here, too, are the familiar tram rails and cobbles. *1-264*

St George's Cross dominated by the huge sign for Massey's Corner in a 1956 picture which also emphasises the ugly web of street wiring needed to cope with a tramway system. *1-265*

(Above): The famous Argyle Street store Lewis's says it with flowers to celebrate the coronation in 1953.
1-266

(Right): Byres Road – the social and commercial heart of the West End as it looked in the late 1950s.   *1-267*

Shop assistants take the sun on the roof of the then Lewis's department store with the old Queen Street station façade in the background. The store is now Debenhams and linked to the St Enoch Centre.   *1-268*

Browsing for book bargains was a favourite hobby of Glaswegians with Renfield Street the site of many of the best barrows. This is 1939 and the threat of war is temporarily forgotten in the search for a good read.   *I-271*

Why the fruit market had to move to new premises – congestion in Candleriggs in the 1950s.   *I-269*

Before the fruit market moved
from Candleriggs the area
around the Ramshorn Church
was crowded with fruit and
vegetable salesmen, their
merchandise, barrows and
lorries. This was the scene on a
summer's morning in May 1949.
I-270

Paddy's Market was so called
because it was the area where
Irish immigrants sold cast-off
clothing. It dates from the
1820s and had various sites
around Shipbank Lane.   *I-274*

Vanilla ice cream, pears – there was no shortage of refreshments or characters in The Barras as this 1940s picture shows. *I-272*

That Glasgow institution, The Barras, is always thronged especially around Christmas time. Here in the 1950s the rival stallholders hawk Christmas merchandise. *I-273*

On the Move

In the 1990s the Kingston Bridge became a controversial structure almost constantly under repair but here in 1985 it spectacularly speeds the night traffic across the Clyde. *I-275*

The Ring Road north of the Kingston Bridge under construction in June 1970. This picture gives some impression of the massive impact of this huge civil engineering project on the centre of the city. *I-276*

Part of Charing Cross in 1974 after the completion of the ring road. In the early days there was an outcry about lack of pedestrian crossings and this picture was especially taken to show how Glaswegians responded by vaulting the railings and walking along the roadway regardless of the danger of fast-moving traffic.   *I-277*

Vehicular Ferry No. 3 is the unromantic designation of the Finnieston Ferry seen here in 1958 snapped between the stern of a freighter and a dredger as it makes its regular way back and forward across the river in the days before the Kingston Bridge helped kill the ferries.   *I-278*

As well as the vehicular ferries the Clyde was crossed by many pedestrian ferries like this one at Whiteinch, looking rather like a scene from a sinister B movie, on a bleak December night in 1963.   *I-279*

This was a black day for young Marjory Bain who along with her mother used the Renfrew Ferry on regular trips to see her grandparents in Clydebank – the fare that had remained at a halfpenny since 1911 was doubled to one old penny in February 1956. At the same time the pedestrian fare on the Erskine Ferry doubled from one penny to two!   *I-280*

This was how the Renfrew Ferry looked at the time of the fare increase. The extra cost was no deterrent to car and lorry drivers who found the few hundred yards across the river much preferable to driving up to a city bridge. *1-281*

The Renfrew Ferry in its refurbished splendour as a concert venue moored at the Broomielaw in the 1990s. *1-282*

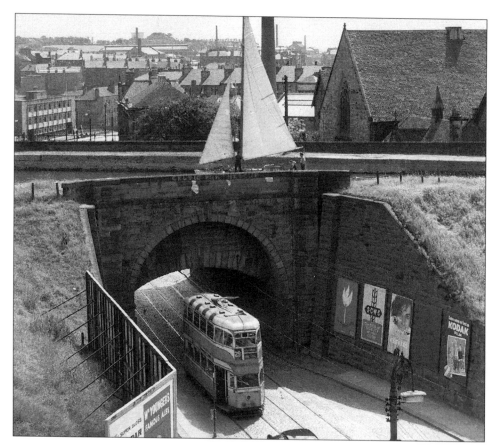

A city yachtsman
heading down the
Forth and Clyde
canal crosses the
Maryhill Road
without a care for
passing traffic in
1961.   *I-283*

The maritime side of Maryhill! This is the Forth and Clyde Canal in the mid 1950s.   *I-284*

Swans on the calm waters of the canal at Port Dundas in the late 1950s.   *1-285*

The old saying had it that Glasgow made the Clyde and the Clyde made Glasgow. But the river required regular dredging to keep it navigable. Dredgers such as the *Craigiehall* pictured in the mid 1950s were a familiar sight to commuters crossing the bridges to work.   *1-286*

In recent years there hasn't been much call for ice-breakers on the Clyde, but here tugs clear a passage for a sailing vessel at Govan in the 1890s. In the background is a ship under construction. *I-287*

The world's last sea-going paddle steamer *Waverley* being towed down the Clyde from Anderston Quay to the former Stephen's dry dock at Govan early in 1976. The steamer's first season after being donated to the Paddle Steamer Preservation Society was in 1975 and she was *en route* to Stephen's for boiler repairs, passing General Terminus Quay which later became part of the 1988 Glasgow Garden Festival site. *I-289*

The Clyde in the 1950s was still servicing a considerable tonnage of shipping. Queen's Dock is on the right. *I-288*

The Clyde has always proved a challenge to engineers. Here is the King George V Bridge under construction in 1924. The original caption remarked that this would be about all sightseers would see for at least a year as all the early work was to be done under water.   *I-290*

Jamaica Bridge in 1955 chock-a-block with trams, single-decker buses, double-decker buses, cars, lorries and pedestrians heading home southward.   *I-291*

The old railway bridge in Great Western Road at Anniesland was a bottleneck for many years. Here a steam locomotive passes overhead as work to widen the road under the bridge goes on in 1936.   *I-292*

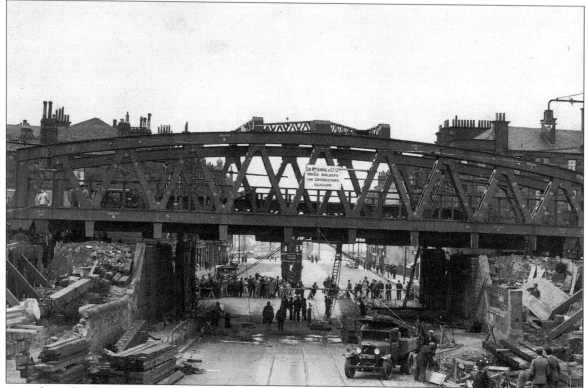

A year later after the widening of the road William Arrol and Company's new bridge is carefully positioned in an effort to improve the traffic flow.   *I-293*

An accident in 1951 caused this jam-up of trams in Paisley Road giving the clippies an extended break.   *1-294*

The early days of the motor car could still produce congestion as this shot of West George Street shows.   *1-295*

St Enoch's Church once stood in the Glasgow square of the same name. By the
time of this photograph the site was providing parking for a fascinating
collection of motor cars. Park in the city centre for free? Changed days indeed.
However, the theme remains… in the present-day use as a bus terminus.   *I-296*

When the trolley-buses arrived in Glasgow they were nicknamed the 'silent death' but they were nonetheless
mourned after their demise. Here is one of the last trolley-buses in action on Saturday, 27 May 1967, their final
appearance on city streets. Inset is a souvenir trolley-bus ticket issued by the Scottish Tramway Museum Society to
commemorate the last day. The trolley-bus service had begun in the city in 1949.   *I-297*

Glasgow's Underground system was closed between 1977
and 1980 for a £55m modernisation which included
rebuilding St Enoch Square station. Originally, access was
by means of the building on the left, which also served as
the headquarters of the subway company. It required
underpinning and is now a travel centre. Behind is the site
of St Enoch railway station and hotel, now occupied by a
shopping centre. The hotel finally fell victim to fire
regulations in 1974.   *I-298*

A pre-1926 picture of St Enoch's Parish Church in St
Enoch Square with a line up of cabs. Interestingly the
roof of the old subway was used to advertise some of
the various destinations.   *I-299*

Perhaps the most distinctive aspect of the Glasgow underground system was the smell of stale air in the stations – something a photograph cannot capture. Here however is the way it looked inside the old subway in the 1960s. Not a 'No Smoking' sign in sight!   *I-300*

Morning rush hour in the subway in 1964 with commuters packed on the narrow platforms.   *I-301*

Parliamentary Road looking west before the demolition of the 1960s.   *1-302*

Blairdardie schoolchildren wait for the early morning bus to take them to Knightswood Secondary School in November 1964.   *1-303*

Before the advent of smokeless fuel and the demise of heavy industry Glasgow suffered severely from fog and smog which could turn daylight into darkness. Here the Maryhill tram looms into view at the junction of Argyle Street and Jamaica Street.　*I-304*

Trace horses at the ready in West Nile Street in the 1940s. These magnificent beasts were ready to give assistance to any carters struggling with the steep hill and the slippy cobbles.　*I-305*

Work on the tram
rails in West Nile
Street in 1953.
I-306

The passing of an
era: the last tram
parade on 4
September 1962
brought
thousands of city
families on to the
streets to say a
fond farewell to
'the shooglies'.
Now in the 1990s
there is talk of
reviving trams as
a way of easing
urban congestion.
I-307

Renfrew Airport got this futuristic new terminal in 1954 but by 1966 it had to give way to the new Abbotsinch Airport. Also the old Renfrew Airport main runway became part of the M8, which provides the road link between the city and its new airport.   *I-308*

There has always been regular traffic between Glasgow and Ireland involving bus, train, boats and planes. Here holiday makers in 1956 leave Renfrew Airport to head out for Ireland.   *I-309*

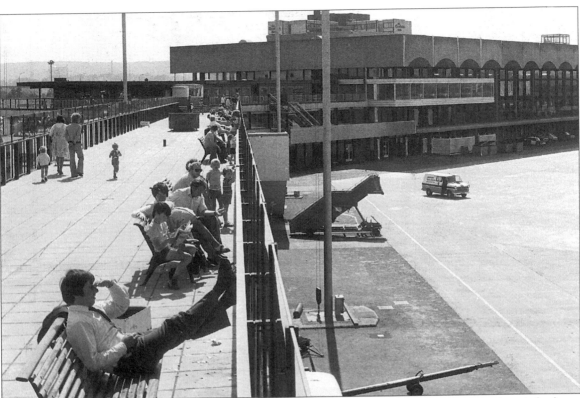

Abbotsinch in its role as a civil airport in the 1980s before the threat of international terrorism put airport viewing areas out of bounds and relegated passengers and spectators to air-conditioned lounges.   *I-310*

Renfrew Airport, Scottish Flying Club, Air Pageant June 1935. Avro 504s in the foreground gave aerobatic displays and stunt flying. DH Dragon in middle of picture and behind it a Cierva Autogyro which was demonstrated.   *I-311*

A fascinating picture of Renfrew at the time of the King's Cup Air Race, September 1922. The two large aircraft are Blackburn Kangaroos which reports suggest did not reach Renfrew during the race. This photograph shows them there.   *I-312*

The legendary Captain David Barclay of Scottish Air Ambulance fame flies a BEA De-Havilland Rapide over its successor, a DH Heron at Renfrew, 15 March 1955.   *I-313*

Two BEA 'Pionairs', converted from Douglas DC3s by Scottish aviation at Prestwick, on the apron at the new passenger terminal at Renfrew, November 1954.   *I-314*

Abbotsinch was used by the RAF and the Royal Navy before taking over from Renfrew as Glasgow Airport. Here in 1960, a glider from an Air Training Corps school scatters press men and spectators as it beats-up the runway, perhaps a little lower than intended.   *I-318*

Air Day at the Royal Naval Air Station, Abbotsinch in July 1960 as a Tiger Moth makes a showy turn above a Blackburn Beverley transport aircraft. Abbotsinch opened as a Royal Air Force station in 1933 specifically for the use of 602 (City of Glasgow) Squadron Auxiliary Air Force, and was transferred to the Royal Navy in 1943.   *I-315*

BEA Viscounts at the new Glasgow Airport at Abbotsinch. In the background is the India Tyres factory at Inchinnan near where Beardmores built the R 34, the first aircraft to complete a double crossing of the Atlantic in 1919. *I-316*

Inauguration of British Airways 'Super Shuttle' service – 30 August, 1983 – three Concordes at Glasgow. *I-317*

Troubled Times

(Left): Blackened iron bars on the exterior of a furniture factory in James Watt Street where 20 people died in November 1968. Firefighters, police and onlookers were helpless as anguished screams came from within the burning building as victims attempted to break free.   *1-319*

(Right): Nineteen firemen died in the infamous Cheapside Street whisky warehouse blaze in 1960. The picture shows the remains of a fire tender after the building's wall blew outwards sending masonry crashing down.   *1-320*

(Left): Owner Reo Stakis outside the ruins of the Grosvenor Hotel in Great Western Road which was badly damaged by fire in 1978. It was later rebuilt with a splendid recreation of the original façade and became once again one of the West End's finest buildings.   *1-322*

(Right): Firemen pour water into the burning St Andrew's Halls through the Granville Street façade which was the only part of the building to survive the 1962 blaze. The Halls were originally built in 1873-77. Now the Mitchell Theatre continues the tradition of music and entertainment on part of the site.   *1-323*

Thirteen shop assistants died in the Grafton's gown shop blaze in Argyle Street in May 1949. A hero of the blaze was Mr Soloman Winetrobe who won the George Medal for saving five girls. *I-321*

Firefighters battle a blaze at the Lyric Theatre in Sauchiehall Street in 1953. The Lyric began life as the Royalty in 1879 and was rebuilt after the fire, but demolished in 1962. *I-324*

When the music had to stop. Brian Nunny, the then general manager of the famous Glasgow music store, Cuthbertson's, sits at a £1,000 piano that had been hired for two weeks but became a victim of the Close Theatre fire at the Citizens' in 1973. *1-325*

The sad end of Garscadden House in Drumchapel, destroyed by fire in 1959. This handsome building was completed in 1747 by William Colquhoun of Garscadden who had bought Drumry from Viscount Garnock. At the time the lands of Drumry had been shorn of the areas of Jordanhill, Cloberhill, Drumchapel and Knightswood, but the acquisition still made the Colquhouns the largest proprietors in what was then East Kilpatrick. *1-326*

Anxious faces at a window as firemen hose down a storage tank at a paint works fire in Dobbies Loan in the 1960s. The number of major fires in Glasgow over a period of years earned it the unenviable nickname of 'tinderbox city'. *I-327*

A sad search for evidence goes on at Stairway 13, the scene of carnage when 66 fans died and 145 were injured at Ibrox on 2 January 1971. Rangers equalised in the last minute after Celtic had taken the lead and the fans racing back upstairs were engulfed by those leaving seconds after the final whistle. *I-329*

Daylight reveals the full horror of the Clarkston disaster in October 1971. Twenty people died in a mid-afternoon gas explosion that blew apart ten shops.　*I-328*

16 December 1987. Demolished. The notorious Hutchie E flats crumble after the *Evening Times* revealed that the eight blocks were riddled with killer brown asbestos. The blocks, built to replace the densely populated Gorbals tenements were first found to be riddled with dampness. They stood empty for eight years until the *Evening Times* shock exposure of deadly asbestos paved the way for the bulldozers.　*I-332*

Children being vaccinated against smallpox in 1950. Glasgow, as a port, suffered from periodic smallpox scares.
I-330

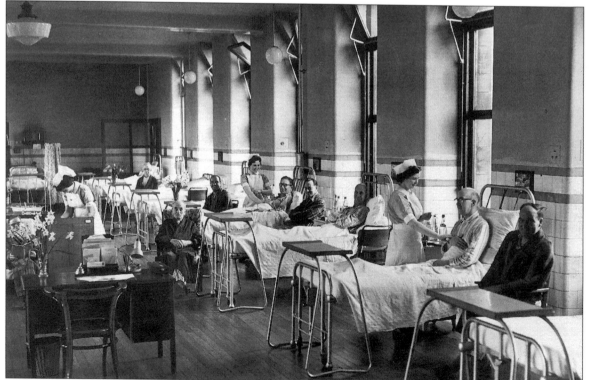

Ward 9 in the Royal Infirmary in the 1950s. The original caption said in this traditional ward that the men can engage in their favourite pastime: "They are terrible chatterboxes," said the nurses, "That is why they do not want to be divided up into small groups in the modern wards". *I-331*

A City at War

George Square in 1919 is bedecked with bunting to celebrate the first anniversary of the armistice of World War One.   *I-333*

Off to war with pipes skirling - soldiers of the HLI-leaving their Main Street, Bridgeton, HQ heading for active service at the front in November 1915.   *I-334*

The HLI-march down Sauchiehall Street into Renfield Street with precision and style. Huge crowds line the city streets to watch the young men of the regiment head for the horrors of World War One.   *I-335*

At the start of World War Two there was a concerted drive to build air-raid shelters. Here Lord Provost Paddy Dollan is seen in 1939 inspecting some of the types on show at the Scottish ARP School for 'instruction in incendiary bombs' at Beech Avenue, Ibrox.   *I-336*

George Square packed for a fund-raising 'Wings for Victory' display in 1943.   *1-337*

The old Ross's Dairy building, a landmark, now demolished, in Crow Road is sandbagged and camouflaged during World War Two.   *1-340*

War fever – this Supermarine Spitfire went on show in the McLellan Galleries in Sauchiehall Street in 1939 as part of the Royal Aircraft Exhibition. *I-338*

King George VI and Queen Elizabeth watch a tank manoeuvre outside the North British loco works in Glasgow during World War Two. This particular picture was, interestingly, subject to censorship. The original caption points out that Censor Number 29 objected to its further use in newspapers after its original appearance.
I-339

In 1941 the fear of a gas attack on the British mainland was still strong. Here, in a rehearsal of what would happen in the event of an attack, a decontamination squad are at work in the Govan streets. *I-341*

As a horse-drawn buggy rumbles past, three Air Raid Precautions women set to with a will to clear snowy wartime streets in 1942. *I-342*

In cold World War Two winters every piece of fuel was vital. Here is the queue for coke outside Tradeston Gas Works.   *I-343*

Solidarity between Scotland and the USSR in 1943 as the Saltire shares centre stage with the Hammer and Sickle at Red Army Day in the old St Andrew's Halls. *I-344*

Parts of a Junkers 88 dive bomber examined in Blythswood Square where the remains went on view to raise money for the City of Glasgow War Relief Fund. *1-345*

Rescue workers hunt desperately for survivors in streets and houses bombed into heaps of rubble. During the two nights of bombing 1,200 Clydesiders died, more than 500 in Clydebank alone. *1-348*

The dreadful scene of devastation in Radnor Street, Clydebank, after the German bombing raid on 13 March 1941. A survey earlier that month showed that only 30 per cent of Clydesiders thought heavy air raids were likely. In the event the unexpectedness of it made the night all the more horrific.   *I-346*

In a picture marked 'passed by the censor for publication' a family of bombed-out Bankies wander the blitzed streets heading for temporary shelter. The devastation caused by the raids left only seven houses intact out of a stock of 12,000.   *I-347*

This partially demolished house in Boyd Street, Govanhill, in 1941 was a major wartime memory for southsiders. Most of the blitz damage was in industrial areas of Clydeside but this unfortunate suburban house was hit by a stray bomb. *1-350*

This 1945 aerial shot shows some of the temporary houses in Dalmuir built for those bombed out in the Clydebank blitz. *1-349*

Bombed out: The sad debris of war litters a Glasgow street during World War Two as the homeless search among their possessions. A particularly poignant touch is the budgie in a cage, a survivor of the bombers! *1-351*

One smiling
clippie reflects the
nation's relief and
joy on the news of
the German
surrender in May
1945.
I-352

Crowds throng George Square to
celebrate the German surrender.   *I-353*

Wartime Prime Minister, Winston Churchill, visited Glasgow in June 1945, weeks after the end of the war, and attracted huge crowds in triumphant mood.   *1-354*

The war has been over for two years but here Spitfires of Glasgow's 602 Squadron exercise in the June skies above Abbotsinch.   *1-355*

Characters and Curiosities

A familiar figure on the streets of Glasgow was Charlie Williamson who was perhaps Glasgow's most famous street musician. He was still going strong in the 1990s when he was almost 80. Charlie once met Yehudi Menuhin and the picture of them together became one of his treasured possessions. The great man admired Charlie's style.   *I-356*

Another of Glasgow's top-class street fiddlers – Alexander Goodwin talks to Glasgow's most famous chronicler, Jack House, pictured outside the *Herald* offices in Buchanan Street in 1961. *I-357*

Buskers have always been part of the Glasgow scene. Here Ivan Inversion – who said he had to sing in short, sharp stints because his act went to his head – entertains in Sauchiehall Street. This Londoner has toured the world busking and described the people of Glasgow as very generous. *1-358*

Ivan Orloff was a well-known East End character whose street strong man act attracted large crowds. At the age of 70 he could still lift three men and a 220lb weight. Originally he was called Martin Breedis and he had been an officer in the Tsar's Royal Dragoons, resigning his commission in 1930 when he came to Britain as a top-rank Greco-Roman wrestler. He served in the artillery in World War Two. *1-359*

'Fivers Watson' was a well-known horse dealer in the city earlier in the century. Here his Gallowgate funeral attracts large crowds, including the inevitable figures 'hingin oot' from upstairs windows.   *I-360*

Three legendary Glasgow characters get together for the Lord Provost's Awards at a 1987 ceremony in the City Chambers. Conductor Sir Alexander Gibson, the journalist and writer Jack House, who had a long-running literary love affair with the city, and former Celtic and Scotland footballer Danny McGrain.   *I-361*

In the 1960s singer Frankie Vaughan got involved with the problems of young gangs in Easterhouse and made a controversial effort to help stop the feuding and help provide much needed facilities for an under-resourced scheme. He became something of an Easterhouse celebrity. Here he made a splash at the scheme's swimming pool.   *1-362*

Johnny Ramensky led a remarkably adventurous life although he spent much of it behind bars because of his safe-blowing exploits. During World War Two he was dropped by parachute behind enemy lines to steal secret documents from safes. He was known as 'Gentle Johnny' because he seldom resisted arrest. He died in Perth Prison, serving a 12-month sentence, in October 1972. Here in 1959 he enjoys his own fireside as a break from prison.   *1-363*

The trial of mass murderer Peter Manuel fascinated the entire city for weeks on end in May 1958. Here crowds gather to watch witnesses arrive at the court. Inset: Manuel – he was convicted of seven murders, later confessing to another three before being hanged in Barlinnie Prison on 11 July 1958. *I-364*

This cormorant was a city centre celebrity around 1977 and 1978 when it made its home on the Clyde just down river from the Carlton Place suspension bridge.   *I-365*

Bud Neil's Lobey Dosser cartoon strip in the *Evening Times* in the 1950s and his pawky Pocket Cartoons drew a huge cult following. *Herald* readers subscribed to a statue of Lobey, his evil enemy Rank Bajin and Lobey's trusty steed El Fidelo which was erected in Woodlands Road in 1992.   *1-366*

Down the years George Square has more or less been permanently at war with starlings. Here Mr Bill McCracken fires off a blank round to scare away the offending birds in 1957.   *1-368*

The taximen's outing to raise money for sick children is an ongoing city tradition. Here a magnificently dressed cab heads out for the coast in 1956.   *I-369*

Here a rag man goes looking for business in the Finnieston area as late as 1964, bugle in hand to attract custom. *I-370*

James Freer of Bridgeton was, in 1951, one of the only two licence holders in the city to take children for pony and trap rides at a penny a time.   *I-371*

The hero of El Alamein, Field Marshall Viscount Montgomery, in his uniform as Colonel-in-Chief of the Royal Warwickshire Regiment helped attract huge crowds at the wedding of his son, David Montgomery, and Miss Mary Connell, daughter of Mr Charles Connell, the Clyde shipbuilder, in St Mary's Cathedral, Great Western Road in 1953.   *I-372*

Tommy Morgan was one of the most loved of all the Glasgow comedians, presiding over a string of successful shows at the Pavilion. Here, on the eve of an international football match, he has a bit of fun with Tommy Lawton of Arsenal and England and George 'Corky' Young, legendary skipper of Rangers and Scotland.   *I-373*

Hard-working women with pramloads of heavy washing arriving at Kingston Baths in 1957. The day of a washing machine in nearly every home was a long way off! But the visit to the steamie was often the occasion for gossip and a good laugh.   *I-374*

The real life steamie shows the accuracy of the set of Tony Roper's highly successful play in the 1990s. This was the washhouse in Kingston Baths in the 1950s.   *I-375*

Through the mangle… an early picture of a Glasgow washhouse.   *1-376*

The George Bennie 'railplane' was an attempt to create a new method of high speed transport. It was expected to achieve speeds of 100 mph and provide an invaluable means of developing rural districts and relieving congested roads in towns. In the event it never got beyond this test track in Milngavie, a few miles north of Glasgow.   *1-377*

Glasgow has always specialised in turning out characters. Here Lizzie Dale, a city centre apple seller, takes time off for a snack in December 1949 but it is tea and a sandwich rather than a bite of her own merchandise.   *I-378*

The People's Palace curator, Elspeth King, made a huge impact on the city and its appreciation of its history. Here she is, left, enjoying a fund-raising stunt in 1987. She considered the museum was starved of cash and threatened to take in washing to raise funds. With her is Mrs Pam Harper, a tour guide at the People's Palace who had helped to hang out the family washing on the Green when she was a girl.   *I-379*